First Pro Game

It was October 16, 1992. Now it was time for Shaquille to show the world what he could do.

To open their exhibition season, Shaquille and the Orlando Magic were in Miami, Florida, to play the Miami Heat. Excitement was in the air. Shaquille's first National Basketball Association game felt more like the playoffs than a pre-season exhibition.

The owner and the front-office staff of the Magic had traveled down from Orlando, Florida, for the game. As Shaquille left his hotel in Miami, there was a crowd outside waiting to get a peek at the 20-year-old who was expected to become the next great player in the N.B.A. Inside the arena was a sell-out crowd of 15,008 screaming fans. Sportswriters from all over the country, along with radio and TV crews, had come to report on Shaquille's first game.

Read all about it and the major events in Shaquille's life leading up to it. How does this awesome athlete deal with fame? Who were the major influences in his life? It's all here in the pages of this **Sports Illustrated for Kids** book, SHAQUILLE O'NEAL.

Shaquille O'Neal

By Neil Cohen

Illustrated by Steve McGarry

A **Sports Illustrated for Kids** Book

Bantam Books
Toronto • New York • London • Sydney • Auckland

SHAQUILLE O'NEAL
A Bantam Book/November 1993

SPORTS ILLUSTRATED FOR KIDS and
are trademarks of Time Inc.
SPORTS ILLUSTRATED FOR KIDS BOOKS® is an imprint of
Bantam Doubleday Dell Publishing Group, Inc.
All rights reserved. Used under authorization.

Cover design by Miriam Dustin
Cover photograph by Manny Millan
Interior illustrations by Steve McGarry

ISBN 0-553-48158-4

Published simultaneously in the United States and Canada.

Bantam Books are published by Bantam Books, a division of Bantam Doubleday Dell
Publishing Group, Inc. Its trademark, consisting of the words "Bantam Books" and the
portrayal of a rooster, is Registered in U.S. Patent and Trademark Office and in other
countries. Marca Registrada. Bantam Books, 1540 Broadway, New York, NY 10036.

PRINTED IN THE UNITED STATES OF AMERICA

0 9 8 7 6 5 4 3 2
CWO

This book is for you, the reader.
Never stop growing. Keep reading, always.

Contents

1

Opening Night

Friday, October 16, 1992, was a big day in the life of Shaquille O'Neal. That evening, he would play in his first game as a professional basketball player in the National Basketball Association. He was just 20 years old.

Shaquille had dreamed about this day since he was 16 years old and a high school basketball player in San Antonio, Texas. He led Robert G. Cole Senior High School to a state championship and was named to the high school All-America team. College coaches from all over the country asked him to play for their schools because they thought he could help them win a National Collegiate Athletic Association championship.

As a college basketball star at Louisiana State University, Shaquille was honored as the best player in the country. Professional basketball coaches hoped he would leave college early—as early as after his freshman year—because they thought he would lead their teams to an NBA championship. When he left college

> Shaquille is one of the biggest men in the NBA, but he is not the tallest. The three tallest players are:
> 1. **Manute Bol**, Philadelphia 76ers, 7'7"
> 2. **Mark Eaton**, Utah Jazz, 7'4"
> 3. **Rik Smits**, Indiana Pacers, 7'4"

after his junior year, the Orlando Magic made him the first pick in the 1992 NBA draft.

Why did everyone think Shaquille would be such a great NBA player? Shaquille plays center, the most important position on the court. The center is usually the tallest player on the team. Like the guards and forwards, he is expected to score points. But his job is also to keep opponents from scoring by rebounding and blocking shots.

At 7'1" and 303 pounds, Shaquille is one of the **biggest men** ever to play center. But he is not just big and strong. He is also a great jumper and as quick as players much smaller than he is. Shaquille was a great rebounder and shot-blocker in high school and college. And no one can keep him from scoring when he gets close to the basket.

Shaquille was already being compared to NBA All-Star centers Patrick Ewing, David Robinson, and Hakeem Olajuwon, and to all-time great centers **Wilt**

Bill Russell was a 6'9" center for the Boston Celtics from 1956–69. He was a great shot-blocker and rebounder. In his 13-year career, he averaged 22.5 rebounds per game, and led the Celtics to 11 NBA championships!

Wilt Chamberlain was a 7'1", 275-pound center for the Warriors, 76ers, and Lakers from 1959–72. Wilt was a great scorer. He *averaged* 50.4 points per game in the 1961–62 season and once scored 100 points in a game (1962)—the most ever in the NBA.

Chamberlain and **Bill Russell.** The Orlando Magic were paying him a salary of almost $6 million a year. Companies that made sneakers, sporting goods, soft drinks, and toys were paying him more money to endorse their products. And he had not even played his first pro game yet!

Now it was time for Shaquille to show the world what he could do.

To open their exhibition season, Shaquille and the Orlando Magic were in Miami, Florida, to play the Miami Heat. Everyone was excited to see Shaquille finally play. The game felt more like a playoff game than a pre-season exhibition.

The owner and the front-office staff of the Magic had traveled down from Orlando, Florida, to watch

Shaquille's first game. There was a crowd outside the Magic's hotel in Miami, waiting to get a peek at Shaquille when the team boarded the bus for the ride to the Miami Arena. Inside the arena, there was a sell-out crowd of 15,008 screaming fans. Sportswriters from all over the country, along with radio and TV crews, had come to report on Shaquille's first game.

"I had butterflies," Shaquille would say later. "I was nervous."

At 7:30 p.m., the game was ready to begin. Shaquille and Miami center Rony Seikaly took their positions in the middle of the court for **the center jump**.

The Heat won the tap and brought the ball down-court to start the game. Shaquille followed Rony as the veteran Heat center looked to test the rookie right away. The crowd buzzed with anticipation. Shaquille was big, all right, the fans seemed to say, but how good was he?

Suddenly, they found out. Rony caught a pass,

Hoop Talk:
The center jump. To start a game, the two centers meet at the center circle in the middle of the court. The referee tosses the ball high in the air between them. Each center tries to tap it to one of his teammates.

drove across the foul lane, and took a shot from about five feet away from the basket.

Normally a shot from that close to the basket is a "can't miss" basket for a player as big as Rony, who is 6'11" tall himself. But not this time. Shaquille leapt into the air, reached out as far as he could with his right arm, and swatted the ball away. The ball landed 11 rows deep, in the courtside seats.

The crowd became quiet. Then they began to buzz again, as fans turned to their neighbors to talk about the great block they had just seen. As the players on the court lined up for the Heat's inbounds play, Magic guard Scott Skiles had a few words for Rony Seikaly. "It's a whole new world now, Rony," Scott told the Miami center.

NBA, meet Shaquille O'Neal!

Throughout the game, Shaquille was a force on defense. If he didn't block a shot, he forced the shooter to change his shot. Miami forward John Salley was so afraid of having Shaquille block his first shot that he panicked and threw it over the backboard.

On offense, however, things were more difficult for

Hoop Talk:
Turnover. When a player on offense makes a bad pass, commits an offensive foul, or is called by the referee for a violation that gives the other team the ball.

Shaquille. The Heat had two men guarding him most of the time. He was confused and made some bad passes. Shaquille had four **turnovers** in the first quarter and didn't score his first NBA basket until late in the period.

In the second quarter, Shaquille began to feel more comfortable. He passed better and got two assists. "He picks things up quickly," said Scott Skiles.

And he scored 11 points. Heat backup center Matt Geiger picked up four quick personal fouls trying to guard Shaquille, and the Magic moved out to a 49–47 lead at halftime.

The Magic held on to their lead in the second half. Meanwhile, Shaquille brought the crowd to its feet again, this time with his hustle. While chasing after a loose ball, he dove into the Heat bench, headfirst.

When the game was over, the Magic had a 107–102 victory. And the crowd got what it came for. Shaquille finished with 25 points—even though he had played just 33 minutes of the 48-minute game. He also had three blocked shots. Plus, his presence in the middle had prevented the Heat players from driving to the basket for easy buckets.

On offense, Shaquille showed that he was powerful but also quick and agile for a big man. He had a nice **shooting touch** and good hands. He also helped his teammates. When he was guarded by two defenders, he tried to pass the ball to the teammate who was unguarded.

> **Hoop Talk:**
> **Shooting touch.** The way a shooter releases the ball. The more backspin, the softer the touch—and the better the chance the ball will go into the basket.

But Shaquille also showed that there was still room for improvement. He made only three of eight free throws. He committed nine turnovers. He got into foul trouble. He also seemed to tire easily; one time he even had to come out of the game to catch his breath.

Still, everyone was impressed with what Shaquille could already do.

"Shaq did some great things," said Matt Guokas, the coach of the Magic. "He's shown every indication of being a special young man."

"Shaq looks like he's going to be an unbelievable talent," said Kevin Loughery, the coach of the Miami Heat.

"You don't realize how talented he is until you play

> **Hoop Talk:**
> **Post up.** When a player has the ball close to the basket, with his back to the basket and the defensive player behind him. This is a good position to score from or to pass the ball out to an open teammate.

against him," added Rony Seikaly. "The first time he **posted up**, I realized how big and strong he really is."

"In all my years," said Magic backup center Greg Kite, "I've never seen a package of talent like his. Patrick Ewing has a lot of strength and David Robinson is really quick, but nobody combines the strength and quickness that Shaquille has."

Shaquille was tired after his first NBA game. He showered and dressed. He stayed to answer the questions of all the reporters who had come to interview him. He spoke softly. He was modest and polite.

He told the reporters that he was satisfied with how he had played, but he knew that this was just the beginning. Tomorrow night, the Magic would play the Heat in Orlando.

"I'm going to go home and think about what I did wrong," Shaquille said. "My mother's going to be there at the game tomorrow, so I'm going to have to get better and play extra hard."

Then he smiled, said good-bye, and headed for the team bus. The reporters smiled back. It was refreshing for them to see a 20-year-old kid that big and that good who loved to play basketball and wanted to play even better. Outside, fans were waiting for another look at Shaquille and calling his name.

"He's a cross," said his agent, "between Bambi and the Terminator."

Shaquille seemed to be having such a great time just being Shaquille O'Neal. But it wasn't always that much fun.

Army Brat

Shaquille O'Neal didn't start out on top of the world. He began his life, on March 6, 1972, in a poor neighborhood in Newark, New Jersey, a city just across the Hudson River from New York City.

Newark had been battered by race riots in July 1967. African-Americans in the city had become angry at not being able to find jobs that paid well and at having to live in neighborhoods filled with crime. They felt that the city was not providing the services they needed to have a safe community. The schools looked like jails. The playgrounds were piles of rubble. The city had no money to improve the schools or to fight crime in these areas, so the local government had no solutions.

Finally, because people were so frustrated, riots broke out in the streets. Stores were looted. Cars were turned over. Fires were set. The National Guard had to be brought in to restore order.

After the riots, things were even worse than they had been before. The buildings that had burned down were not rebuilt. Shopkeepers boarded up their looted stores and moved away. And the people tried to carry on.

One of the few bright spots in the community was the work of the **Black Muslims**. The Black Muslims were a religious group who tried to teach black men and women to have pride in their heritage and not to depend on the white community for their own success. They also urged African-Americans to get a good education and to stay away from drugs, alcohol, and crime.

Some African-Americans in Newark converted to the Islam faith and became Muslims themselves. But many who didn't convert still admired the work of the Muslims and gave their children Muslim names.

Shaquille's parents, Philip Harrison and Lucille O'Neal, were not Muslims, but they respected what the

Black Muslims are members of a religious movement in the United States called the Nation of Islam. Its members believe that the true religion of African-Americans is Islam, the religion of Asia and Africa. Black Muslim leaders stress the need for black people to be independent of white people. In the 1950's and early 1960's, the most important spokesman for the Nation of Islam was Malcolm X.

Muslims were trying to do. They lived in a housing project in Newark. Sometimes they had to depend on food stamps to buy groceries.

Mr. Harrison had dropped out of college. Ms. O'Neal had finished high school and become pregnant with Shaquille. Just before their son was born, Mr. Harrison joined the United States Army, hoping to build a better life for his family. But before he could marry Ms. O'Neal, he was sent away to an Army base for training..

Both of Shaquille's parents were big. Mr. Harrison was 6'5". He had been a basketball player in junior college and, for a time, in college. Ms. O'Neal was 6'2". They expected Shaquille to be big, too. When Shaquille was born, the first thing his father did was send home a new football uniform.

Shaquille's parents gave him the Muslim name Shaquille Rashaun. Shaquille's mother wanted her children to have unique names. "Just having a name that means something makes you special," she said.

In the Islamic language Shaquille means "little one" and Rashaun means "warrior." Shaquille's name means "little warrior." Shaquille was given his mother's last name because his parents were not yet married when he was born.

As soon as the Army allowed him to go home, Mr. Harrison returned to New Jersey and married Shaquille's mother. But Mr. Harrison still wanted his son to keep his mother's last name. Mrs. Harrison had no brothers or nephews to carry on the O'Neal family name. Mr. Harrison felt that was important and he wanted Shaquille to be the one to do that.

Shaquille's dad became a staff sergeant in the Army. He was transferred to a different base every few years, and the family moved with him. Over a period of 10 years, they moved from New Jersey to Georgia, back to New Jersey, to Germany, back to New Jersey, back to Germany again, and finally to San Antonio, Texas. They lived on the base, and Shaquille went to school with the children of other soldiers.

Meanwhile, the Harrison family was growing. Shaquille's sister Lateefah was born when he was 5. His sister Ayesha was born the next year, and his brother, Jamal, the year after that.

When Shaquille was 10, Sergeant Harrison was transferred to an Army base in Wildflecken, Germany. This time, Shaquille didn't want to leave New Jersey. "He wanted to stay there with his grandma," his father remembers.

Shaquille still considers Newark his hometown, but today he is glad he left the city when he did. "There were a lot of temptations—drugs, gangs," he says. "The best part for me was just getting out of the city."

But having a dad in the Army was a hard life for a kid. Shaquille would have to leave his friends and make new ones. Then he would have to leave his new friends

When Shaquille was 10 years old, in 1982:

* The Smurfs were a popular cartoon show on TV.

* The University of North Carolina (led by Michael Jordan) won the National Collegiate Athletic Association men's basketball championship over Georgetown University (led by Patrick Ewing).

* Americans first became aware of the disease AIDS.

* Michael Jackson's *Thriller* became the best-selling album of all time.

* The first space shuttle mission was launched.

and make new ones again. "We'd stay for a couple of years and then move on," he says. "I didn't ever really have a best friend."

It was even harder for Shaquille because he was having trouble fitting in with the other kids. He was growing fast. He was 6'5" by the time he was 13 years old. He wasn't well coordinated. He was clumsy and he slouched all the time, trying to look shorter. "My parents told me to be proud of being so tall," Shaquille remembers. "But I wasn't. I wanted to be normal."

His parents had trouble finding clothes for him. Stores rarely had his size. When they did, he couldn't wear the clothes for long. "We'd buy him pants on Saturday and by the next Friday they wouldn't fit," recalls his dad.

With his size, bad posture, and too-small clothes, it was hard for Shaquille to make new friends. The kids on the Army bases would make fun of him. "I always got teased," says Shaquille. "Teased about my name. Teased about my size. Teased that because I was so big I must have been left back a grade in school.'"

Shaquille would get mad and hit the kids who made fun of him. "That made it even harder to make friends," Shaquille adds, "because people thought I was mean."

One way Shaquille tried to get kids to like him was by taking dares, doing wild things, and being the class clown in school. But that only got him in trouble with his parents. As a drill sergeant, Sergeant Harrison's job was to teach recruits discipline. He demanded the same kind of respect at home.

One time, a classmate at the base school dared Shaquille to pull the fire alarm at school. Shaquille did. Two fire trucks and several police cars came, all with their sirens on. The MPs, or military police, who keep order on an Army base, took Shaq down to the police station on the base. Sergeant Harrison had to be called to the station to take Shaquille home. He was angry at Shaquille and punished him.

Another time, Sergeant Harrison dropped in at

school and caught Shaquille and the other kids dancing around the classroom and banging chairs together instead of sitting and listening to their teacher.

When he asked Shaquille why he was acting that way, Shaquille said it was because the other kids were doing it.

"You've got to be a leader, not a clown," said his dad. "We got enough clowns." And he punished him again.

Still another time, at home, Shaquille found a cigarette lighter and set his teddy bear on fire. When his mother came home, he put the fire out and threw the bear under his bed. His mother found the blackened teddy bear. This time, she did the punishing.

Shaquille was always getting into trouble. "One time, my parents punished me for a whole year," he says. "All I could do was go to school and come home."

His dad was strict, Shaquille says, but now he understands why. "He taught me right from wrong and to treat people the way I wanted to be treated myself," Shaquille says. "He's the kind of person that when he tells you to do something, you do it. I had to find out the hard way."

His mother taught Shaquille that he didn't have to get into a fight with everyone who looked at him strangely. She would listen to him complain about being teased and say, "A man would just say yeah, and walk away."

One day, Shaquille decided he had had enough of getting in trouble. He wanted to do things differently. "I finally got tired of being punished and tried it their way," he says. "And it worked."

Shaquille was still big and clumsy. But he started walking away from fights. He still liked to have fun, but he stopped doing things that would bother other people. He worked harder in class and at making friends.

He also started playing more baseball, basketball, and football at the recreation center on the Army base. His coach was his dad. But Shaquille wasn't very good at sports.

What he really loved was dancing. "The funniest thing," says Shaquille, "is that I never really wanted to be a basketball player. I always wanted to be one of those guys in the movie *Fame*."

Shaquille loved to break dance and could even spin on his head. But then he became too big and too wide to do those fancy moves.

One day he picked up a basketball and looked at it in a whole new way. Here was something he could do and be proud of his size instead of frustrated by it. Basketball could be Shaq's chance at a great life. But there was lot of work to do first.

3

From Hoop Horror to Hoop Heaven

It's hard to believe that Shaquille O'Neal wasn't always a monster on the basketball court. But when Shaquille was 13, he was more like a mouse. Even his mother says so. "He was wimpy," she remembers.

Shaquille was big, but he did not have a lot of natural talent for basketball. He was clumsy and he couldn't jump at all. During a game, he didn't want to be passed the ball because he was afraid he would drop it or throw up a wild shot. His friends teased him all the time.

"I was awkward," he remembers. "I fell down a lot. God only gave me, I'd say, 48 percent athletic ability. I had to work for the other 52 percent.

"I couldn't always run. I couldn't always shoot. I couldn't always dunk. I had to practice. I don't believe in talent. I believe in working hard."

One day, while the family was living in Germany, Shaquille went to a basketball clinic given on the Army base by Dale Brown, head coach of the men's basketball team at Louisiana State University (LSU). Coach Brown liked to travel around the world, giving basketball clinics and looking for student athletes who might want to go to college at LSU.

After the clinic, Shaquille asked the LSU coach for advice.

"Coach Brown," he said. "I need a strength program for my legs because I'm 6'5" and I can't jump."

Coach Brown looked at this tall young man and asked, "How long have you been in the Army, soldier?"

"I'm not in the Army," Shaquille answered. "I'm only 13."

Coach Brown was surprised. Then he looked at Shaquille's feet. "What size shoe do you wear?" he asked.

"Seventeen," Shaquille replied.

Coach Brown thought for a minute. He knew that a 13-year-old with feet that big had a very good chance of growing even taller. And he knew how much a big center could help his basketball team. "Can I meet your father?" he asked eagerly.

Even though there were still four years before Shaquille would be ready for college, Coach Brown wanted Shaquille and his dad to start thinking about LSU right away.

Coach Brown went to find Sergeant Harrison, who

was relaxing in the base's sauna. Coach Brown was so eager to meet him that he stepped right into the hot sauna in his street clothes.

Coach Brown told Sergeant Harrison that Shaquille would grow to be a seven-footer. He also said that if Shaquille became a good basketball player, he would like him to consider attending LSU.

Sergeant Harrison put up his hand to stop Coach Brown from talking. He told the coach that he wanted Shaquille to become not just a good basketball player, but a good person. "Playing basketball is fine," he said. "But I'm more concerned with this young man's education. If you're still interested, maybe we'll talk someday."

Coach Brown wiped the sweat off his face and smiled. "Sergeant," he replied, "we're going to get along just fine."

After Coach Brown returned from his trip to Germany, he found a letter on his desk. It was from Shaquille. He had written to say he wanted to hear more about LSU. For the next four years, Coach Brown sent Shaquille and his family loads of articles, booklets, and letters about LSU.

One day, soon after the visit by Coach Brown, Shaquille was shooting baskets alone at an outdoor court on the base. He had never been able to dunk, but he thought he'd give it another try. He drove toward the basket, jumped, and . . . *slam!* He dunked the basketball!

"It was a weak dunk," Shaquille remembers, "but I was so excited I had to tell everybody."

Shaquille's friends didn't believe that he had dunked. So he brought them to the court to watch him do it again. But this time he couldn't.

Everybody walked away. "You can't dunk, man," somebody said.

Shaquille continued to get teased by his school-mates. In ninth grade, he tried out for his school bas-ketball team but was cut. The coach told him his feet were too big and his movements were too clumsy. But Shaquille kept practicing and working with his father. He did exercises to strengthen his knees, ankles, and thighs. His dad taught him some moves from his days as a college basketball player.

"I learned how to never give up," Shaquille says. "I just kept practicing every day. When everybody was going to parties, I was outside dribbling, working on my coordination, and trying to dunk."

Shaquille practiced so that he could jump quickly and get a head start to the ball. He worked on his rebounding so that he could judge on which side of the basket a missed shot might come down. And little by little, he began to jump higher and higher.

Shaquille's favorite players were **Kareem Abdul-Jabbar** and **Julius Erving**. But his father told him not to try to be like another player, but to develop his own style of play.

"That stuck with me," Shaquille says today. "I didn't

> **Kareem Abdul-Jabbar** was the 7'2" center for the Milwaukee Bucks and Los Angeles Lakers from 1969–88. Kareem is the NBA's career scoring leader (38,387 points). He played on six NBA championship teams and was named MVP six times. His most famous shot was the sky-hook, which he shot down on the basket.
> **Julius Erving** was a 6'6" forward for the Nets and the 76ers. His nickname was Dr. J. Julius was a great scorer and leaper, and was known for his spectacular dunks. He played on three championship teams, won four MVP awards, and averaged 20 or more points for 14 straight seasons.

want to try to be somebody else. I wanted my own identity. I wanted to be a complete player. An aggressive player. One who hustles all the time. One who is sportsmanlike. And, most of all, one who is a winner."

By the time he entered tenth grade in the American School on the Army base in Germany, Shaquille was playing well enough to make the school team.

In 1987, when Shaquille was 15, his dad was transferred back to the United States. This time, the family moved to San Antonio, Texas, where his father was stationed at Fort Sam Houston.

Shaquille's parents enrolled him at Robert G. Cole

Senior High School in San Antonio, which was near the Army base. Most of the students at the school had parents who were in the Army.

Shaquille had no problems fitting in at his new school, especially after he showed what he could do on the basketball court. Shaquille really began to blossom as a player after he arrived at Cole.

"A lot of kids come in from Germany, and they have these big stats that don't mean anything," says Dave Madura, Shaquille's coach at Cole. "Shaq, though, could do everything he said he could do."

By now, Shaq had grown to be 6'9" tall. He started wearing uniform number 33 in honor of Kareem Abdul-Jabbar. Shaquille played mostly a power game as a center. He would catch the ball near the basket, then dribble and **back in** against his opponent for an easy shot. Or he would grab the rebound of a teammate's missed shot and put it into the basket. Although he could jump higher now—his **vertical leap** was 18"—and had gotten quick for someone so big, Shaquille scored most of his points because he was so big and strong that none of the other high school centers could stop him.

In his junior year, Shaquille led the Cole Cougars all the way to the semi-finals of the state championship tournament. Everyone expected Cole to go all the way. After all, the tallest player for the opposing team, Liberty Hill High School, was just 6'3". Unfortunately, Shaq let those predictions give him a swelled head.

> **Hoop Talk:**
> **Back in.** When a player turns his back on a defender and dribbles the ball as he moves backward and closer to the basket for a shot.
> **Vertical leap.** How high a player can jump straight into the air from a standing start.

"I'm going to score 50 points," he told a sportscaster for the local TV station. "Nobody on earth can stop me."

Shaquille was so sure that Cole would beat Liberty Hill that he stayed out late the night before the big game.

It didn't turn out the way Shaquille had planned. Liberty Hill came out shooting jump shots from way outside—and making them! Shaquille committed four fouls in the first two minutes and had to sit on the bench for the rest of the quarter. Liberty Hill jumped out to a 21–2 lead.

Cole came back, however, and the Cougars were down by just one point with five seconds left to play. Shaquille, who had only eight points, was fouled. He went to the line to shoot two free throws that could win the game for Cole—and he missed them both! He was very upset with himself. "That was the last time I ever said that I was bigger than anyone," he remembers.

In his senior year, Shaquille led Cole to a 36–0 record and a state championship. He averaged 32.1 points per game and was named a high school all-American. Over the two years that Shaquille played at Cole, the Cougars won 68 games and lost only one game. Shaquille averaged 32 points, 22 rebounds, and 8 blocked shots per game.

After the season, Shaquille was invited to play in the McDonald's High School All-America game in Kansas City, Missouri. The game featured the best high school players in the country and was shown on national television. Shaquille showed he belonged in this group of high school stars. He scored 18 points and had 16 rebounds, as his West team beat the East team.

On one play, Shaquille wowed college scouts when he grabbed a rebound off one backboard and dribbled it the length of the court to dunk in the other basket. Shaquille was named one of the game's most valuable players, along with the East's Bobby Hurley. Bobby, who played for St. Anthony's High School of Jersey City and who went on to be a star player for Duke University, set an all-star game record with 10 assists.

By then, Shaquille had become the most sought after college recruit in the country—just two years after he had returned from Germany. More than 100 college coaches contacted Shaquille and offered him an athletic scholarship if he would play for their school.

Some coaches tried to impress Shaquille with the

number of players they had sent on to the NBA. Other coaches promised him that he would start on the team right away. Others said they would get him on the cover of *Sports Illustrated*.

But Shaquille wanted to go to LSU. Coach Brown had written Shaquille regularly since they had met four years earlier. He had also come often to watch him play—before any other coaches had even heard of Shaquille. It showed Shaquille that Coach Brown had believed in him from the start.

Sergeant Harrison told Coach Brown that Shaquille would be there all four years, no matter what the pros offered. "If blacks are to get a piece of the American pie," Sergeant Harrison said, "we should get an education."

When Shaquille's college choice was announced in the newspapers, many people thought that Sergeant Harrison had made the decision for his son. But the sergeant set that straight.

"That was him alone," he said. "We pushed the boat away the day he decided to go there. We told him, 'Go out there and take what we taught you and what you have learned in life and apply it to do what you have to do.' "

4
The New Kid

Shaquille arrived on the Louisiana State University campus in the fall of 1989 to begin his freshman year of college. It was the first time he had ever lived away from his family, and he was homesick. He called home a lot to talk to his mom and dad.

LSU is in Baton Rouge, Louisiana, which is a seven-hour drive from San Antonio, where Shaquille's family lived. Every weekend he could, Shaquille made the long drive home to see his parents, sisters, and brother. When the season began, his family drove to Baton Rouge every weekend that the Tigers had a home game to watch him play.

In the classroom, Shaquille decided to major in business. Even though he hoped to play in the NBA someday, he didn't know if he'd be good enough to make it, and he wanted to have a career he could fall back on. If he did become a professional basketball player, studying business would help him learn how to handle his money.

Shaquille settled into dormitory living. Dormitories

are buildings on campus where students live while they are attending college. Shaquille decorated his dormitory room by hanging posters of NBA stars on the walls and a pair of fuzzy dice in the doorway.

Sports fans in Louisiana really support their college teams, especially LSU basketball. The LSU Tigers sell most of the seats in the 14,164-seat **Pete Maravich** Assembly Center, the arena where they play their home games. Fans were expecting big things from the Tigers in the 1989–90 season.

Along with Shaquille, the team had two other star players. Chris Jackson was a sophomore guard who had averaged more than 30 points per game and been named to the All-America team as a freshman. Stanley Roberts was a sophomore center/forward who was also 7' tall and a good shooter. One sports magazine even picked LSU to win the national championship!

Pete Maravich played guard for LSU from 1967–70. He was the greatest scorer in NCAA history. He holds the records for most points scored in a season (1,381, for 44.5 points per game) and in a career (3,667, for 44.2 per game). His nickname was "Pistol Pete."

Shaquille and Stanley became good friends. They guarded each other at practice and talked about playing against each other in the NBA someday.

Shaquille also spent a lot of time lifting weights to get stronger for the start of the season. The team's strength and conditioning coach said Shaquille worked so hard that sometimes he would find him on the floor of the weight room, rolling around in pain.

Like most of his teammates, Shaquille decided to play with a **T-shirt underneath his LSU jersey**. That had become the style in college basketball. He had to wear a gold T-shirt under his gold "home" jersey and a purple T-shirt under his purple "road" jersey. NCAA rules stated that the T-shirts had to be the same color as the jerseys. Shaquille kept the number 33 he had worn in high school, to honor Kareem Abdul-Jabbar.

LSU was a member of the Southeastern Conference (SEC), one of the most competitive conferences in col-

The first player to wear a T-shirt under his uniform jersey was **Patrick Ewing**, when he played for Georgetown University. Patrick was born in Jamaica, where the weather is warm most of the time. He wore the T-shirt because he was cold during games at air-conditioned arenas.

lege basketball. The SEC is made up of 11 universities, most of which are located in the southeastern portion of the United States. When the season began, Shaquille learned that college basketball was a lot tougher than anything he had seen in high school.

For one thing, it was harder to score. In high school, he would just back in against smaller kids for a dunk or a lay up. He had never needed to learn to shoot a jump shot or a hook shot. His strength had been enough. Now, he was being guarded by bigger and stronger players.

For another thing, the college defenses were a lot trickier. Sometimes opposing players would **double and triple team** Shaquille when he got the ball close to the basket. He would become confused and make a bad pass or commit an offensive foul.

The other players were a lot better than high school players, too. Shaquille was overeager to block shots, and opposing players would often fake him out. That got him into **foul trouble** in a lot of games. Shaquille **fouled out** of nine games in his freshman year.

What made things even tougher for Shaquille was that the Tigers were not playing as a team and passing the ball to each other. Chris Jackson was both the point guard and the team's leading scorer, averaging almost 28 points per game. That means he dribbled the ball downcourt and ended up taking most of the shots himself.

> **Hoop Talk:**
> **Double teaming or triple teaming.**
> When a player is guarded by two or three
> defensive players.
> **Foul trouble.** When a player commits a lot
> of fouls early and must sit on the bench until
> his team really needs him.
> **Foul out.** In college basketball, each player
> is allowed to commit five personal fouls
> before he must leave the game. In the NBA,
> players are allowed six fouls.
> **Fadeaway or fall-away.** A shot taken by a
> player as he is leaning back, away from the
> basket, to prevent the shot from being
> blocked.
> **Paint.** Another name for the area within the
> foul lane. It is usually painted in one of the
> home team's colors.

"It was a very difficult year for me," Shaquille says. "Coach Brown's philosophy was: If you're open, shoot it. And Chris was so quick that every time he touched the ball and made a move he was open. So he shot it most of the time. The only time I got the ball was on rebounds. Most of my shots were **fadeaways** in the **paint** with a hand in my face."

When Chris wasn't shooting the ball, it seemed, Stanley was. He was the team's second leading scorer, with 14 points per game. Shaquille, on the other hand, got 15 or more shots in a game only three times. He made the most of his shots, though, and scored 20 points or more five times.

Shaquille didn't complain about not getting enough shots. He knew that if he was patient, his time would come. In the meantime, he concentrated on rebounding, playing good defense, and blocking shots. He twice had 20 or more rebounds in a game. He blocked 115 shots for the season, which set an SEC record. Against Loyola-Marymount University, Shaquille had an awesome defensive game. He blocked 12 shots and grabbed 24 rebounds.

But the season was a disappointing one for LSU. The team that had been picked by some basketball experts as one of the best in the country won 23 games and lost 9 during the regular season.

After their regular season ends, most conferences hold a tournament to determine a conference champion. The conference champion (plus other teams from the conference) then moves on to play the other top teams in the country in the National Collegiate Athletic Association tournament. The winner of the NCAA tournament is crowned national champion.

But LSU had no more success in the post-season tournaments than it had during the season. The Tigers lost in the first round of the SEC tournament to Auburn University. Then they lost in the second round of the

National Collegiate Athletic Association (NCAA) tournament to Georgia Tech University.

Coach Brown blamed himself. "That year, I did the worst job of my entire 34 years of coaching," he said later. "I thought the time had finally come when I could sit back and watch my players play. I got sloppy and my team reflected it."

Still, by doing his job, Shaquille had made the most of his freshman season. He was named to the All-SEC team and the freshman All-America team. He averaged 13.9 points and 12 rebounds per game. And he had done it while scoring well in the classroom, too. Shaquille had a 2.90 grade point average out of a possible 4.0 (that's a B average) as a business major.

His style of play had also made him popular with the fans. A husband and wife in Geismer, Louisiana, even named their new baby after Shaquille. When Shaquille found out, he drove to Geismer to visit the parents and have his picture taken with the baby.

Soon after the season ended, Chris Jackson decided to leave LSU to play in the NBA. He was drafted in the first round by the Denver Nuggets. Stanley Roberts also left school early, to play pro basketball in Spain.

Coach Brown knew that the team's future was in Shaquille's hands. So he named Shaquille co-captain of the team, even though Shaquille was just 18 years old and one of its youngest players.

That summer, Shaquille was invited to play on the South team in the Olympic Festival basketball tournament, a competition for some of the best college players in the country. Coach Brown was the coach of the South team.

Shaquille was determined to use this trip to make an impression on the court. For the first time since he had started playing college basketball, he was going to be the main man, the center of attention.

He went to work right away to show what he was capable of doing when he got the basketball. In the first game, Shaquille's South team defeated the West team 112–100. Shaquille scored 26 points, grabbed 10 rebounds, and blocked 10 shots. It was the first **triple double** in the history of the festival!

The next night, in a 128–121 loss to the North team, Shaquille scored 39 points to set a tournament record. He also had 14 rebounds and 7 blocks, and stopped the game for 15 minutes after he ripped the rim off the backboard on a big slam dunk.

When the tournament was over, Shaquille had set a new scoring record for the Olympic Festival and helped win a gold medal for the South team. For the first time since he had arrived at LSU, Shaquille felt he was playing the way he should. "I'm 7'1", 285 pounds," he said. "Seven feet means dominance."

On the victory stand, after the final game, each player on the winning team was given a bouquet of

A **triple double** is a game in which a player has 10 or more points, rebounds, and assists, or 10 or more points, rebounds, and blocked shots. Magic Johnson, who played guard for the Los Angeles Lakers from 1979–91, had 136 triple doubles (points, rebounds, and assists) in his NBA career. Oscar Robertson, who played guard for the Cincinnati Royals and the Milwaukee Bucks from 1960–74, averaged a triple double for a season in 1961–62 (30.8 points, 12.5 rebounds, and 11.4 assists per game).

flowers. Afterward, a little girl ran up to Shaquille to ask for his autograph. He gave her an autograph *and* the flowers. "I love kids," he explained later to a reporter. "Maybe because I still am one."

Sportswriters at the Olympic Festival were amazed by what Shaquille had been able to do against the best college players in the country. But Coach Brown told them they had only seen a little of what Shaquille could do. "Shaq has unlimited ability," he said. "He's like a newborn colt. This is just the beginning."

5
Shaq Attack!

When Shaquille returned to LSU in September for the start of his second year of college, basketball fans were still buzzing about his play at the Olympic Festival. Pro scouts said Shaquille was ready to play in the NBA now!

But Shaquille didn't want to think about any of that yet. He just wanted to enjoy being an 18-year-old college kid. And off the court, that's just what he was.

Shaquille enjoyed playing Nintendo video games and **listening to rap music**. He liked to play disc jockey in his dorm room, mixing music from side-by-side turntables. He told reporters that if he weren't a basketball player, he'd want to be a comedian or a rapper. He had a lot of friends, both on and off the team, and because of his name, he had a lot of nicknames.

Like most 18-year-olds, Shaquille's favorite clothes were a baseball cap, T-shirt, jeans, and sneakers. The difference was that Shaquille had to buy his clothes in a big and tall men's store and have his size 19 sneakers made just for him.

Shaquille's favorite things:
* Rap group: Fu-Schnickens
* Singers: Al B. Sure and Stephanie Mills
* Movie Star: Eddie Murphy
* Cartoon character: Heathcliff
* Animal: Doberman pinscher
* Food: Chicken
* Activity (besides basketball): Sleep

Basketball practice began on October 15. There was less pressure on the Tigers in 1990. With Chris Jackson and Stanley Roberts gone, LSU was not expected to win the national championship. Most sports experts thought the Tigers would finish no better than fifth or sixth place in the SEC.

Coach Brown changed the team's game strategy so that the offense revolved around Shaquille. The guards were told to look for Shaquille first when they brought the ball downcourt and pass the ball to him if he was open. If he didn't have a good shot, Shaquille was told to pass it out to a teammate for an outside jump shot.

When the season began in November, Shaquille picked up where he had left off at the Olympic Festival. In a win over in-state rival Southeastern Louisiana University, Shaquille scored 28 points, collected 11 rebounds, and had 6 blocked shots. Against the University of Texas, he had 26 points, 18 rebounds, and 5 blocks.

But it was a game in December that showed the whole country just how good a player Shaquille had become. LSU was playing the University of Arizona on national television at the Maravich Center. The Arizona Wildcats were ranked Number 2 in the country and had won their first seven games. The Wildcats had a lot of big players, including 6'11" Sean Rooks, 6'11" Brian Williams, and 7' Ed Stokes. They were considered the best center-forwards combination in the country.

Shaquille had to sit on the bench for much of the game because of foul trouble and a pulled stomach muscle. But with six minutes left to play, he came back into the game and took over.

He scored 16 points down the stretch, rattling the backboards with his slam dunks. After one dunk, he even did a little dance—right on TV!

LSU beat Arizona 92–82. Shaquille scored a career-high 29 points and had 14 rebounds, 6 blocked shots, and 5 steals.

"I wanted to dominate the game," Shaquille said. "I was always taught, 'It's your court. You rule it and you control it.'"

Even Arizona coach Lute Olson was impressed. "There's no question Shaquille is the best center in the country," he said.

Shaquille was getting better and better. But Shaquille and Coach Brown knew there was still plenty of room for him to improve. So Coach Brown asked **Bill Walton** and Kareem Abdul-Jabbar, two of the greatest centers in basketball history, to come to Baton Rouge and work with Shaquille.

Bill had led the University of California at Los Angeles (UCLA) to two national championship titles in the 1970's and the Portland Trail Blazers to an NBA title in 1977. He was a great passer. He worked with Shaquille on his passing, on his footwork, and on how to stay out of foul trouble.

Kareem had been one of Shaquille's heroes when he was growing up. He had led UCLA to three national championship titles in the 1960's and had won 6 NBA titles with the Milwaukee Bucks and the Los Angeles Lakers in the 1970's and 1980's. Kareem is the NBA's all-time leading scorer. He helped Shaquille with his jump shot and hook shot.

Bill Walton was a 6'11" center who was known for his passing and his defense. Bill led the Portland Trail Blazers to an NBA title in 1977 and played on a championship team with the Celtics in 1986. He won the league's most valuable player award in 1978.

Shaquille worked on all those things in practice. Then he put them to use in games. He was becoming unstoppable. In a 98–74 win by LSU over Arkansas State, Shaquille had a career-high 53 points. After the Shaq attack rolled over Nicholls State, 118–76, the opposing center said, "I felt like I was guarding the Washington Monument."

Shaquille liked to show people that even though he was more than 7' tall, he could do more than dunk, rebound, and block shots. Against Auburn University, he brought the ball downcourt with a behind-the-back dribble, then passed to a teammate for a layup. Against the University of Alabama, he threw an over-the-head, no-look pass to another teammate for a dunk.

Shaquille tried not let his success go to his head. "I'm a pretty good player," he said, "but I don't think I'm the best." Rival coaches, however, thought he was awesome.

"He's a combination of David Robinson and Hakeem Olajuwon," said Kentucky coach Rick Pitino, comparing Shaquille to two NBA All-Star centers. "He's 295 pounds of grace."

"He's like a man among boys," added Arkansas coach Nolan Richardson.

Shaquille was having a lot of fun. Each home game at the Maravich Center had become a big party. There were indoor fireworks and an appearance by Mike V, the Bengal tiger that is the LSU mascot.

The number of reporters from newspapers, magazines, TV, and radio who wanted to interview Shaquille had grown and grown as the season went on. Within a three-day period, Shaquille was featured on the covers of two national sports publications.

Shaquille didn't like to read what was written about him in newspapers and magazines. But he tried to be courteous and friendly with reporters.

"I realize I'm different," Shaquille said. "I can handle it all one of two ways. I can be nice and talk to reporters, or walk around and be arrogant. What fun would that be?"

Shaquille's face had been on TV and in magazines so many times that people began recognizing him in airports when he traveled with the team. He thought about buying a mask so that no one would recognize him. Coach Brown had to laugh. "Here's a guy who is 7'1", 295 pounds," he said, "and he thinks he can go around unnoticed."

LSU was scheduled to play Duke University in early February, and everyone was looking forward to the showdown between Shaquille and the Blue Devils' great center, Christian Laettner.

The game was played at Duke's Cameron Indoor Stadium. Christian was 6'11" and weighed 240 pounds, but he looked tiny next to Shaquille. Duke, however, was a much better all-around team than LSU. They were on their way to winning the first of two straight national championships.

The Blue Devils played good team defense and kept the other Tigers from passing the ball to Shaquille, who only got nine shots in the game. Meanwhile, Christian showed what a good outside shooter he was. He kept Shaquille off-balance by mixing up his drives to the basket with long outside shots.

Duke won easily, 88–70. Christian led everyone with 24 points and 11 rebounds, while Shaquille was held to 15 points and 10 rebounds.

At the end of the game, the Duke fans started teasing Shaquille. "One, two, three, four," they chanted. "Shaquille can't play no more."

Shaquille didn't get mad; he thought it was funny. "I wanted to laugh," Shaquille told reporters after the game. "But we were down by 18."

Even though they had teased him, the Duke fans were waiting for Shaquille outside the arena to ask for his autograph. Even Christian was a Shaquille fan. "People don't realize how big he is because of how well he moves," he said. "I consider myself a good-moving big guy, but it's fun to watch him."

Shaquille had been lucky to avoid any injuries in his college career so far. But in LSU's next-to-last regular season game, fate caught up with him: he fractured his left leg in a game against Florida. He missed the Tigers' last regular season game and the first game of the SEC tournament. Without their big man, the Tigers lost both.

Shaquille wanted very much to play in the NCAA

tournament. He told the team doctors that he felt "99.99 percent" and they gave him the go-ahead.

But LSU had to face a tough University of Connecticut team in its first game. Shaquille's leg just wasn't as strong as he hoped it would be. He moved slowly on the court and had to drag his leg behind him. He got tired quickly. Connecticut won the game, 79–62.

Shaquille's season was over. But what a season it had been! Shaquille became the first player ever to lead the SEC in scoring (27.6 points per game), rebounding (14.7 per game), field-goal percentage (62.8 percent), and blocked shots (140) at the same time. He led the country in rebounding and set a record for most blocked shots by a sophomore (he averaged 5.0 per game).

Shaquille was named SEC Player of the Year and a first-team All-America. He won the **Adolph Rupp Award**, given by the Associated Press to the best college player in the country. He also won the Tanqueray Amateur Athletic Achievement Award, which included a $5,000 prize. He donated the money to the Boys and Girls Club of Newark, New Jersey.

Now everyone was wondering if Shaquille would leave school early and enter the NBA draft. Some people estimated that Shaquille could earn as much as $30 million from salary and product endorsements if he turned pro.

Shaquille wanted to join the NBA. He told his par-

The **Adolph Rupp** Award is named for the man who coached the University of Kentucky from 1931–72, won four NCAA titles, and is the all-time NCAA leader in wins (875). The two other major college player of the year awards are also named for coaches. The **James Naismith** Award is named for the man who invented basketball in 1891, when he was an instructor at a YMCA in Springfield, Massachusetts. The **John Wooden** Award is named for the man who coached UCLA from 1949–75 and once won 10 national titles in 12 seasons.

ents that he wanted to buy a house, cars, and nice clothes for them, and toys for his brother and sisters.

But his father told him it was wrong to leave college just for the money. "I want you to go ahead and get a degree so you can be something other than a basketball player," said Sergeant Harrison. "The money will be there when you're ready."

Shaquille's mother said she wanted him to get his college degree more than she wanted a new house, cars, or nice clothes. "That's the most important gift you could get me," she told him.

So Shaquille announced that he would be back at

LSU for his junior year. When kids asked him for his **autograph**, he would sign his name and add the words, "Listen to your mother."

These are a few of the nicknames team-mates, friends, and other LSU students called Shaquille and he called himself: "Sugar Shack," "Love Shack," "Shaq Daddy," "Shaquille the Real Deal," "The Shaqnificent," and "Shaq-Attaq" (on his license plates).

6
Baton Rouge Blues

Shaquille wasn't going to the NBA yet. But he did get to make a special trip. In the spring of 1991, he was invited by President and Mrs. Bush to visit the White House. Mrs. Bush thanked him for setting a good example for children in the United States by staying in school.

After he finished final exams, Shaquille returned home to San Antonio. He spent the summer trying to become an even better player so that he would be ready for his professional career. He practiced his dribbling and worked on his shooting. He added a hook shot and a jump shot from farther away from the basket.

"Last year I was only able to do power stuff," he explained. "But when I go into the NBA, I'll be playing against guys **my size** who are stronger than me—and quicker." Shaquille also played basketball with his younger brother, Jamal. Jamal, who was 12, had already grown to 5'11"! "Everything I learn, I teach him," Shaquille said. "He's going to be a good one."

Sizing up Shaquille:
* Shoes: Size 20
* Shirts: Size 52
* Shorts: Size 48
* Hand: 9" wide and 11" long
* Body fat: 10 percent

When he returned to school in the fall, Shaquille concentrated on his schoolwork. He was on track to make the dean's list. That's an honor roll for college students who have a B average for a semester.

Basketball practice started in October, and Shaquille showed Coach Brown how much he had learned over the summer. Coach Brown was impressed by Shaquille's shooting and ball-handling. He said he had never seen a player who was already very talented improve so much. Coach Brown even added a play to the Tigers' offense in which Shaquille would help the guards by dribbling the ball upcourt against a **full-court press**.

Hoop Talk:
Full-court press. When a team plays tough defense all over the court to prevent the other team from bringing the ball downcourt by forcing a turnover.

LSU fans were expecting the Tigers to do very well this season. LSU was ranked the Number 6 college team in the country. The Tigers had two new players on the team who were good outside shooters: guard Jamie Brandon and forward Clarence Ceasar. Coach Brown hoped that better outside shooting by the rest of the Tigers would keep teams from double teaming Shaquille.

But when the season began, LSU started slowly. In their opening game, at home, the Tigers had to come from way behind to defeat Northeast Louisiana, 77-76. Soon after that, they were beaten badly by the University of Arizona and the University of Nevada-Las Vegas.

Shaquille scored just 15 points against Northeast Louisiana. He was held to 10 points, 4 rebounds, and 3 blocked shots by Arizona. After their first five games, the Tigers were a disappointing 3–2.

The LSU players were not used to playing together. They also were not hitting their outside shots, which left opponents free to concentrate on Shaquille. Whenever Shaquille caught a pass, he was surrounded by three or four defenders. In addition, Shaquille thought he was getting fouled a lot, but the referees weren't making the calls.

That frustrated him. "I feel like I've improved, but I can't really showcase my talent," he told a reporter. "I'm a better passer. My hook move is better. But what can you do with one guy on each side of you? One of them pushes you in the back and the one in the front pulls on your jersey. It's pretty tough."

But Shaquille also wasn't playing with his usual enthusiasm. At times, his attention seemed to wander to the NBA. Late in the loss against Arizona, he said to Wildcat center Sean Rooks, "I don't care how good you play. I'm still the number one draft pick."

Some opponents said Shaquille was playing as if he were trying not to get hurt. NBA scouts wondered if the college game was still challenging enough for him. Shaquille was taking fewer shots each game and only going after the easy blocks so that he would stay out of foul trouble. He was making fewer than half of his free throws.

Shaquille didn't think he was trying any less. But he heard differently from his family. When he went home for Christmas, his dad made him sit down and watch some games he had videotaped. Then Sergeant Harrison got angry at Shaquille "for playing too nice."

Shaquille's grandmother called him from New Jersey. "She had seen a game where I wasn't doing too much," said Shaquille. "She said, 'I saw you play last year, yelling, dunking, hanging on the rim, and diving on the floor. Now you're playing cool.'"

Shaquille got the message. And he knew that he had better get his act together—fast! "In '92," he said, "the Shaq has got to be back."

And he was. In a 74–53 win over 14th-ranked

Hoop Talk:

Fast break. When the offensive team tries to rush the ball downcourt for a shot before the other team has a chance to set up its defense.

Kentucky, Shaquille had 20 points, 20 rebounds, and 6 blocks. On one play, he stole the ball from a Kentucky guard and dribbled the ball downcourt on a **fast break**. At one point, the Tigers won seven games and 10 of their next 11.

But Shaquille wasn't doing it alone. The other players had gotten to know each other and were playing better, too. The guards and forwards were shooting better. That meant other teams couldn't keep double and triple teaming Shaquille.

"Some people think we're a one-man team," Shaquille said. "They haven't realized yet that there's a lot more out there than me. I don't need to score 29. As long as LSU is winning, I'll be happy."

But because the Tigers were playing better as a team, everyone was scoring more—including Shaquille. He increased his scoring to 24.5 points per game. He was also averaging 4.7 blocks and 14.2 rebounds, which was tops in the country.

The Tigers finished the regular season at 19–8. Their 10–3 record in conference games was good for second place in the SEC Western division, just behind the University of Arkansas.

The Tigers still had a chance to win the SEC Tournament, which began right after the regular season ended. LSU had not won a game in the tournament in three years. Shaquille wanted very much to change that.

In the first game, LSU played the University of Tennessee. The Tigers were leading the Volunteers by 22 points in the second half and were well on their way to a victory. Then Shaquille drove to the basket for a slam dunk and was fouled hard by Tennessee forward Carlus Groves.

All the pushing and shoving that he felt opponents were getting away with finally got to Shaquille. Instead of walking away from a possible fight, as he had learned to do as a kid, Shaquille pushed Carlus. He and Carlus started fighting. Soon all the players on both teams started fighting, too. It took the referees 20 minutes to stop the brawl.

Shaquille and Carlus were thrown out of the game, which LSU still won easily. But college basketball frowns on fighting, and Shaquille was suspended for the next game. That was the tournament semi-final game against the University of Kentucky. Without Shaquille, the LSU Tigers were pussycats. They were easily knocked out of the tournament.

Shaquille was very upset. He went to the bank, took

out all his money—$400—and flew home to San Antonio. "After the Tennessee game, I made up my mind to enter the NBA draft," he says. "My dad wanted me to stay in school. But he and mom said, 'It's your life, your decision.'"

Shaquille didn't tell Coach Brown or his teammates of his plans. The NCAA tournament was next, and Shaquille still hoped to win a national championship for LSU.

The Tigers' first game of the tournament was out in Boise, Idaho, against Brigham Young University. Shaquille and company got off to a fast start. Led by Shaquille's triple double—26 points, 13 rebounds, and 11 blocks—they defeated the BYU Cougars, 94–83. His **11 blocks were a record** for an NCAA tournament game.

Two days later, LSU went up against Indiana University. This was a big game. Indiana was one of the

Shaquille was the shot-blocking king of college basketball. He led the nation in blocked shots his junior year with 5.2 per game. He blocked five or more shots in 20 of 30 games (and 45 times in 90 games in his career).

toughest teams the Tigers would have to face on their way to a national championship. The Hoosiers were coached by Bob Knight, one of the winningest coaches in college basketball history.

Shaquille played his heart out. He scored 36 points, pulled down 12 rebounds, and blocked 5 shots. But he was no match for a very strong Indiana team. Led by forwards Calbert Cheaney and Allan Henderson, the Hoosiers won, 89–79.

It was a disappointing time for Shaquille. He had decided his college career was over. He had averaged 21.6 points and 13.5 rebounds per game in three seasons at LSU. He was named SEC Player of the Year and a first-team All-America for the second time. He was runner-up to Duke's Christian Laettner for the John Wooden and James Naismith player of the year awards. But he had not been able to win a national championship.

Shaquille waited to announce his decision to leave LSU and **enter the NBA draft**. He wanted to tell Coach Brown first.

After the tournament, Shaquille went home to San Antonio. He invited Coach Brown to come out for a weekend and talk with Sergeant and Mrs. Harrison. Their house on the base still had a purple and gold LSU flag hanging in the window.

Shaquille's parents tried once again to talk him out of leaving school. They wanted him to be the first per-

Shaquille likes being around family. Here are (from left) his dad, Sergeant Philip Harrison, his mom, Lucille, Shaq, his sisters, Ayesha and Lateefah, and his brother, Jamal.

At Louisiana State University, Shaquille wore number 33 to honor one of his sports heroes, Kareem Abdul-Jabbar.

John Biever/Sports Illustrated

When Shaquille was in college playing for the LSU Tigers, he averaged 21 points and 13 rebounds per game!

Shaquille, at 7' 1" and 303 pounds, stands out wherever he goes, even among the skyscrapers of New York City!

Barry Gossage

Shaquille works on strengthening and stretching his leg muscles to keep up with the grind of the NBA schedule.

Barry Gossage

In his first regular season game, Shaquille showed
he belonged with the pros in the NBA by pulling
down 18 rebounds against the Miami Heat.

Tennis star Aranxta Sanchez-Vicario sizes up Shaquille's warm-up pants and one of his sneakers (size 20!).

SHAQUILLE WAS ONCE A CLUMSY 13-YEAR-OLD WITH BAD KNEES WHO COULDN'T DUNK ... *EVEN THOUGH HE WAS 6'5" TALL !*

WHEN **SHAQ** WAS 13, HIS DAD, AN ARMY SERGEANT, WAS TRANSFERRED TO A BASE IN **GERMANY**. **SHAQ** WENT TO A CLINIC GIVEN ON THE BASE BY **DALE BROWN**, HEAD BASKETBALL COACH AT **LOUISIANA STATE UNIVERSITY** ...

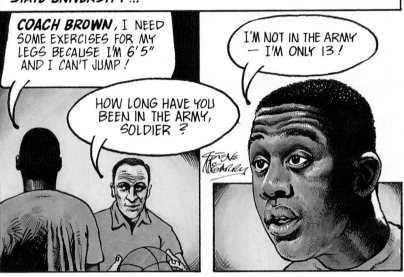

COACH BROWN, I NEED SOME EXERCISES FOR MY LEGS BECAUSE I'M 6'5" AND I CAN'T JUMP !

HOW LONG HAVE YOU BEEN IN THE ARMY, SOLDIER ?

I'M NOT IN THE ARMY — I'M ONLY 13 !

COACH BROWN WANTED TO MEET **SHAQ**'S FATHER, **SGT. HARRISON**. **SHAQ**'S DAD WAS RELAXING IN THE BASE'S SAUNA. **COACH BROWN** WAS SO EAGER TO TALK TO **SHAQ**'S DAD THAT HE STEPPED INTO THE SAUNA IN HIS STREET CLOTHES !

YOUR SON IS GOING TO BE 7' TALL ONE DAY AND IF HE GROWS AS A PLAYER I'D LIKE HIM TO COME TO **LSU**.

PLAYING BASKETBALL IS FINE, BUT I WANT **SHAQUILLE** TO GET A GOOD EDUCATION. IF THAT'S WHAT YOU WANT FOR HIM, TOO, THEN MAYBE WE CAN TALK SOMEDAY.

WHEN **SHAQUILLE** WAS 15, HIS FATHER TRANSFERRED TO **TEXAS** AND **SHAQ** ENROLLED IN **ROBERT G. COLE HIGH SCHOOL**. BY THE MIDDLE OF HIS JUNIOR YEAR HE HAD BECOME A QUICK PLAYER DESPITE HIS SIZE...

HE REALLY **CAN** DO EVERYTHING HE SAID HE COULD!

SHAQUILLE LED HIS HIGH SCHOOL TEAM TO A 36-0 RECORD AND A **STATE CHAMPIONSHIP** IN HIS SENIOR YEAR. IN A NATIONALLY TELEVISED ALL-STAR GAME HE WAS SHOWN GRABBING A REBOUND, DRIVING THE LENGTH OF THE FLOOR AND SLAM-DUNKING!

SHAQUILLE O'NEAL CAN REALLY MOVE FOR A BIG MAN !!!

HE'S GOT A LOT OF COLLEGES TRYING TO RECRUIT HIM !!!

COACH BROWN HAD WRITTEN **SHAQUILLE** REGULARLY SINCE THEY MET FIVE YEARS EARLIER. WHEN IT CAME TIME TO CHOOSE A SCHOOL **SHAQ** CHOSE **LSU**.

LSU WAS ALWAYS MY FIRST CHOICE.

YOU ARE ON YOUR OWN NOW, SON. JUST DO THE BEST THAT YOU CAN DO!

SHAQ BECAME THE TOP COLLEGE PLAYER IN THE COUNTRY. IN 1992 HE WAS THE No. 1 PICK IN THE **NBA** DRAFT.

SHAQ THEN LED THE **ORLANDO MAGIC** TO THEIR BEST SEASON EVER. HE WAS EVEN ELECTED TO START IN THE **NBA ALL-STAR** GAME!

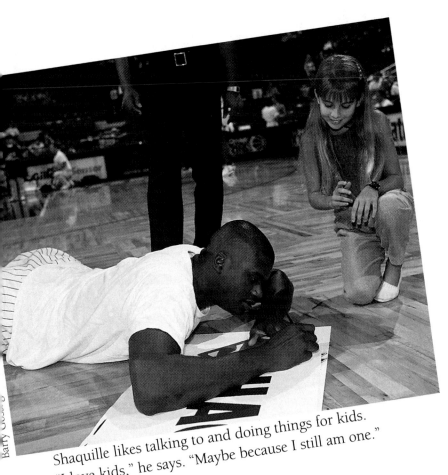

Shaquille likes talking to and doing things for kids. "I love kids," he says. "Maybe because I still am one."

Shaquille was the first rookie to start in the All-Star Game since Michael Jordan started for the East in 1985!

Manny Millan

Shaquille scored 14 points and had 7 rebounds in his first
All-Star Game, which the West won, 135–130.

Shaquille appeared in a Reebok commercial with basketball greats (left to right) Bill Walton, Wilt Chamberlain, Coach John Wooden (seated), Bill Russell, and Kareem Abdul-Jabbar.

Bill Frakes/Sports Illustrated

Shaquille is already one of the most popular and famous athletes in sports. And he's still only 21 years old!

Enter the NBA draft early:
Before 1971, NBA teams would not draft college players until their class (those students who entered school in the same year) had graduated. That rule was changed to allow players whose families had financial problems to leave school early and become professional players so that they could earn money to help their families.

son on either side of the family to graduate from college. Shaquille promised them that he would continue to take classes during the off-season and get his degree after he joined the NBA.

"Shaquille says he will get his degree later, and he usually does what he says he will do," his mom said later. "But I know that later has never come for me. I've always regretted not getting my college degree. I know there's all that money out there, but I want him to have that diploma so he'll have something real to depend on."

But even though they disagreed with his decision, Shaquille's parents were proud that he had been able to make his choice in a mature way. "He didn't do it because he wanted to be rich," his father said. "He weighed all the factors and decided that the best thing for his happiness and his career was to move on. You raise your children to be independent enough to make their own choices, and that's what Shaquille did."

On April 3, Shaquille and his parents held a press conference to announce that he would pass up his senior year at LSU to enter the NBA draft.

"My dad told me at a young age, if you're not having fun at what you're doing, it's time to do something else," Shaquille told the reporters. "And this year I didn't have much fun.

"The experience of going to college was very much needed," he added, "but now I'm ready to take what I learned on with me to the NBA."

7

Fantasyland!

It didn't take long for Shaquille to become a celebrity.

Right after he decided to leave college to become a professional basketball player, Shaquille's family hired an **agent** to represent him in contract and endorsement negotiations. The agent they chose was Leonard Armato, a lawyer from Los Angeles, California, who also represented Kareem Abdul-Jabbar and Houston Rockets center Hakeem Olajuwon.

In May, Leonard brought Shaquille out to Los Angeles to show him around the city. Shaquille appeared on NBC's *Inside Stuff* program.

An **agent** helps a player with his business dealings. He sits down with the team president or general manager to work out how much the player will be paid. He also makes deals with companies who want to use the player to promote their products.

Shaquille's show business career started with a bang. On *Inside Stuff*, he played one-on-one with the show's host, Ahmad Rashad. Shaquille backed in on Ahmad, jumped up, and dunked the ball. The problem was, Shaquille came down with the rim still in his hand. Shattered glass from the backboard went flying all around him.

"I've broken a couple of rims before, but that was my first backboard," Shaquille said. NBC showed the replay over and over again. If any of the people watching TV didn't know what a powerful player Shaquille was before, they knew it now.

Everybody expected Shaquille to be the first pick in the NBA draft on June 24, but nobody knew which team would have the opportunity to select him. On May 17, the NBA held its annual lottery to determine the order in which teams would pick in the draft.

The lottery is set up to give the teams with the worst records the best chance at winning. Ping-Pong balls with the names of the 11 teams that didn't make the playoffs are put into a machine. When the machine is turned on, air is pumped in, and one of the Ping-Pong balls is blown to a small hole in the top of the machine. The team whose name is on that ball gets the first pick of the draft. In this way, the lottery determines the **first five picks of the draft**. The rest of the order goes according to win-loss records, from worst to best.

Shaquille knew he would be going to a losing team,

The all-time greatest NBA draft, say scouts, probably was the 1984 draft. That draft included **Michael Jordan, Charles Barkley, Hakeem Olajuwon, John Stockton, Alvin Robertson, Sam Bowie, Sam Perkins, and Kevin Willis.**

but he didn't mind. "I'm just going to be happy to play," he said. "I've always dreamed about playing in the NBA."

The 1992 lottery was held at the Meadowlands Arena in Secaucus, New Jersey. Eleven NBA general managers sat at a table in front of a television camera as NBA commissioner David Stern announced the lottery results. To keep everyone in suspense, he worked backward, starting with the team that would be drafting eleventh, then tenth, then ninth... Finally, there was just one team left: the Orlando Magic. The Magic had won the lottery!

Pat Williams, general manager of the Orlando Magic, smiled as if he had just won a TV game show. Then, to show everybody how the team planned to use the number one pick, he held up a Magic jersey with "O'Neal" already printed on the back.

The **draft** itself wasn't held until the following month. It took place on June 24 at Memorial Coliseum in Portland, Oregon. Shaquille flew to Portland with his

The 1992 NBA draft featured many great players. Besides Shaquille, some of the other top picks were **Alonzo Mourning** of Georgetown (by Charlotte), **Christian Laettner** of Duke (by Minnesota), **Jimmy Jackson** of Ohio State (by Dallas), **LaPhonso Ellis** of Notre Dame (by Denver), and **Tom Gugliotta** of North Carolina State (by Washington).

agent on the morning of the draft, but he didn't leave his hotel room until it was time for the draft to begin. He wasn't being superstitious; he was just being practical. "I didn't want to get hit by a car," he said.

Meanwhile, on the other side of the United States, the Magic fans in Orlando couldn't sit still. More than 8,000 of them came to the Orlando Arena for a big draft party.

Finally, the moment arrived. Commissioner Stern stepped up to the microphone to announce the first pick of the draft. "The **Orlando Magic**," he said, "select Shaquille O'Neal of Louisiana State University."

The audience in Portland applauded politely. But the crowd in Orlando, watching the draft on TV, hooted and hollered as if they had just seen the Magic win the NBA championship.

The next day Shaquille and his family flew to

Orlando is a city in central Florida. It is best known as the location of Disney World. When the city was awarded an NBA franchise, a local newspaper had a contest for fans to pick a name for the team. The winner, inspired by Disney World's Magic Kingdom, came up with the name Magic.

Orlando to meet the Magic's fans. About 500 people came to the airport to welcome him.

Shaquille got off the plane wearing Mickey Mouse ears with "Shaquille" stenciled on the back. He stepped up to a microphone and said he was looking forward to "chillin' with Mickey" Mouse, now that he would be near Disney World in Orlando. He made everyone laugh when he borrowed his father's glasses and did an imitation of Commissioner Stern announcing his name at the NBA draft the night before.

"I feel fortunate to get picked by Orlando," Shaquille told the crowd. "I'm not promising we'll win a championship in the first year. Things take time. But I'll learn the ropes, get my feet wet, and become a good player."

Shaquille's agent had already arrived in Orlando on the overnight flight to begin negotiating Shaquille's contract with general manager Pat Williams.

Thanks to Leonard's negotiating, Shaquille already

was a millionaire. Many companies were eager to sign Shaquille on as a spokesperson to help sell their products. Shaquille already had an agreement with a sneaker company for Shaquille O'Neal basketball shoes, a sporting goods company for a Shaquille O'Neal basketball, and a toy company for a line of Shaquille O'Neal action figures. Soon, he would also have an agreement to endorse a brand of soda. Shaquille even had his own logo—a picture of a player slam-dunking—that would be used on all Shaquille O'Neal products. All together, these companies would pay Shaquille $15 million a year to promote their products!

After doing a couple of radio call-in shows, Shaquille left Orlando and went home. He spent the rest of the summer flying back and forth between San Antonio and Los Angeles.

Out in Los Angeles, Shaquille spent five days at a special basketball camp for NBA centers and forwards. It was run by Pete Newell, a former NBA coach, who specialized in working with taller players. Shaquille was about to sign a huge NBA contract, but he was still trying to improve his game, especially his footwork, his moves around the basket, and his passing and outside shooting.

At Coach Newell's camp Shaquille had played with a lot of NBA players. Chris Dudley of the New Jersey Nets, Charles Smith of the New York Knicks, Sam Perkins of the Los Angeles Lakers, and Duane Causwell of the Sacramento Kings all took turns guarding Shaquille. But no one was able to stop his slams. "Whoa," said Chris Dudley when he was asked about the new kid, "he dunks on 10-foot rims like they were 8 feet high."

"He's already the best center in the league," added Ken Norman, forward for the Los Angeles Clippers. "He's an overwhelmingly powerful monster."

Coach Newell was impressed by how hard Shaquille was willing to work. "There's a lot of very good players who are satisfied to be good," he said. "But to be a truly great one, you can't be satisfied. Look at Michael Jordan. At one time, he wasn't a very good shooter. Now you can't walk away from him.

"Shaquille wants to be good and he's very receptive to teaching," Coach Newell went on. "If it's going to make him better, he's interested."

Back in Orlando, Leonard Armato and Pat Williams were working 18 hours a day on a contract for Shaquille to play for the Magic. Leonard wanted Shaquille to be the highest-paid player in the NBA. The Magic wanted to sign Shaquille quickly so that the organization could get to work on building the rest of the team around him.

In early August, the deal was completed. Shaquille leaned on top of a piano in a room of the Omni Hotel in Orlando and signed the biggest contract in the history of team sports! Neither Shaquille nor the Magic would say for sure, but reporters estimated that the contract would pay Shaquille $40 million over seven years and $3.5 million in his rookie season.

Both sides were happy that the deal had been done without any name-calling in the newspapers or hard feelings. "If we display the type of teamwork we displayed during contract negotiations, we should be able to make something happen in Orlando," said Shaquille.

Even though he was rich now, Shaquille was still a kid. The first thing he did to celebrate when he got home to San Antonio was take two of his friends to a water park. He even bought them swimming trunks. They all piled on top of the same raft—with Shaquille at the bottom—and went scooting down the slide. "It was a wild ride," said Shaquille.

With the help of his father, Shaquille bought a big house in a suburb of Orlando. Shaquille would live in the house alone until his father retired from the Army in 1993. Then the whole family would move in.

Shaquille bought himself a ring with a huge diamond S in the middle and a gigantic leather coat with an S on the back. On both, the S was in the shape of the Superman logo. And he bought cars. Shaquille had a Mercedes-Benz with a license plate that said "Shaqnificent," a Chevy Blazer with a license plate that said "Shaq-Attaq," and a Ford Mustang that he was going to give to one of his sisters when she was old enough to drive.

But he insisted that money would not change the type of person he was. "Money doesn't make people change," Shaquille said. "People make people change, and I'm not going to let that happen. The only difference money makes is material things. It just means a couple more cars and leather jackets."

Shaquille planned to use his money for other things, too. He wanted to have his grandmother's house in Newark fixed up and to put a cousin through college.

He also wanted to help poor people in Orlando. He purchased 20 season tickets to Magic games to give to kids whose families couldn't afford to take them to a game. He set up a foundation called "Athletes and Entertainers for Kids." Shaquille hoped other celebrities in Florida would work with him. "I want to take some homeless people to a fancy restaurant one night," he said. "I'm going to take 30 kids from poor neighborhoods to Disney World, give them $100 each and let them have fun."

Shaquille went back to Los Angeles in August to play more basketball, this time in pickup games organized by former Los Angeles Lakers star Magic Johnson. Magic had retired from the NBA a few games into the 1991–92 season when he learned he had contracted the HIV virus, which causes AIDS. But he had played in the NBA All-Star Game and with the 1992 U.S. Olympic team.

Every summer, Magic Johnson sponsored a basketball game featuring NBA stars to raise money for the United Negro College Fund, which helps African-American students pay for college. This year, Shaquille was invited to play.

To get in shape for the season and for Magic's game, the NBA stars played every morning at the University of California at Los Angeles (UCLA). Shaquille took these workouts very seriously. "The most impressive thing about Shaquille is that he's such a mature person," said the Knicks' Doc Rivers. "We started at nine o'clock in the morning, and he was there right on time every day. You don't see many college kids like that."

The benefit game drew a big crowd and lots of celebrities to the UCLA Great Western Forum. Arsenio Hall and Spike Lee were the coaches of the two teams.

Even though Shaquille was playing against stars he used to watch on TV, he was cool. He was relaxed and confident on the court, and he put on a show. Shaquille blocked shots by catching them with one hand. He bounced the ball off the backboard on one play and then slammed it through the basket. He spun down the lane for a dunk, while winking at Leonard Armato's four-year-old son in the stands. Shaquille finished with 36 points and 19 rebounds—and he wore everybody out.

"That Shaquille," said Magic, after the game, "he's going to be one of those guys that after you play him, you sleep real good."

Shaquille went home to San Antonio and then on to Orlando to wait for training camp to begin in October. He settled into his house. He tried to go out to a water park and to Disney World for some fun. Everywhere he went, there were fans wanting to shake his hand and get his autograph.

Everyone was expecting great things from him. As Donnie Walsh, president of the Indiana Pacers, said, "I don't think the guys in our league are ready for this guy."

8
Shaquille Goes to Camp

Reporting to your first training camp is a lot like going to your first day of school. When Shaquille showed up at the Orlando Magic's training facility at Stetson University in De Land, Florida, on October 12, he wanted to make a good impression on his coaches and teammates.

Shaquille had done his homework and studied the Orlando Magic's history. For example, he got a smile from point guard Scott Skiles because he knew that Scott held the NBA record for most assists in a game (30).

He also knew that forward Terry Catledge had worn number 33 during his three seasons with Orlando and that Terry didn't want to give up that number—even though team president and general manager Pat Williams had promised it to Shaquille after the draft. "A number's not important," said Shaquille. He took number 32 instead.

"Shaquille could have come in here and been a jerk and there would have been nothing any of us could have done about it," said Scott Skiles. "But he's been just the opposite and that will help make him better and us better."

The big rookie center also made fans of his teammates when he showed them what kind of athlete he is. On the first day of practice, every player on the Magic had to run for 12 minutes around the track at nearby De Land High School. Everyone was given a time he was expected to run. And if someone didn't meet his goal, he had to run it again.

The coaches told Shaquille to run at a pace of 7 minutes per mile. That was a good speed for a 7'1", 303-pound man. But Shaquille surprised everyone by running even faster. He completed his run at a 6:45-minutes-per-mile pace!

At the team's first practice, Shaquille showed the Magic what he could do on a basketball court. During an intrasquad scrimmage, he made some smooth offensive moves, including a spin to the basket and a jump shot from long range. He played with a lot of heart, diving head-first for a loose ball like a baseball player sliding into second base. He slam-dunked and blocked shots, once catching the ball in one hand as if it were a softball.

Hoop Talk:
Scrimmage. A practice game between members of the same team.
Traveling. A rules violation that happens when a player takes steps without dribbling the basketball.

But on the last play of the **scrimmage**, Shaquille got his teammates really excited. He came running down the floor on a fast break, took a pass from Scott Skiles, and seemed headed for a slam dunk. But then veteran center Mark McNamara, playing defense, stepped out in front of him.

Shaquille could have collided with Mark for a foul, or he could have gotten his feet tangled up trying to avoid him and been called for **traveling**. Instead, he kept his cool and made a nifty pass back to Scott for a layup. Shaquille was showing he could do a lot more than slam-dunk!

The Magic's first practice with Shaquille ended with a lot of happy faces. There were high fives all around. Head coach **Matt Guokas** was smiling, too. "He's even more talented than I thought he would be," he said of his newest player.

The Magic already had other talented young players. Scott Skiles, 6'1", is a clever point guard. Dennis Scott is a 6'8" forward with a deadly outside shot. And

Matt Guokas, the Magic coach, played with Wilt Chamberlain and coached Moses Malone. He is also part of the only father-son pair to have played on NBA champisonship teams. Matt senior was on the Philadelphia Warriors team that won the first NBA title in 1947. Matt junior was on the Philadelphia 76ers team that won the title in 1967.

Nick Anderson, at 6'6", is a good scorer who could play both guard and small forward.

With the addition of Shaquille, many Orlando fans were beginning to think the team would make the play-offs and maybe win an NBA championship in his first year. Team president Pat Williams tried to calm them down. After all, the Magic had won only 21 (out of 82) games the season before and just 73 games in their first three seasons. "We should be better," he said. "But we're not ready to win a championship yet."

Shaquille also ignored talk about him winning the Rookie of the Year award or playing in the All-Star Game. "I just want to win and have fun," he said. "Whatever Coach Guokas wants me to do, I'll do."

Coach Guokas told Shaquille what his role on the team would be. He wanted his big man to rebound, block shots, and score around the basket. And he wanted Shaquille to use training camp to learn how to play in the NBA.

"Everyone wants to compare him to Wilt Chamberlain and Bill Russell and Patrick Ewing and David Robinson and Hakeem Olajuwon and all these people," said Coach Guokas. "He's still got a lot to learn, and no matter how much you try to tell any rookie, including Shaquille, they have to learn these things for themselves."

Shaquille was eager to learn. He was always one of the first to arrive at practice and among the last to leave.

In the NBA, basketball is much more physical than even the toughest play Shaquille had seen in college. All the players are so good that they could probably score any time they wanted to. So, in order to give defensive players a chance, referees let them get away with a little pushing, blocking, and holding. That's even more true for centers, who are usually the biggest guys on the team. Big men use their bodies a lot to try to stop, or at least slow down, the player with the ball.

The Magic had invited NBA veteran Mark McNamara to training camp to teach Shaquille about playing center in the NBA. Mark had been a backup center on several teams. He did not have a lot of natural talent, but he really studied the game.

On the first day of practice, Mark told Shaquille, "If

there's anything you want to know, just come to me." And every day, Shaquille kept coming to Mark with questions that got more and more complicated. He was learning quickly.

Greg Kite, the Magic's backup center, was given the job of working with Shaquille in practice. Greg showed Shaquille how to use his body to muscle opposing centers around and keep them off-balance, and how to hold and push when officials aren't looking.

During one very physical practice, Greg was bumping Shaquille around pretty hard. Shaquille turned to Greg and asked, "Why are you doing this to me?"

Greg answered, "Because I like you. I'm going to make you ready for the NBA."

His teammates were impressed to see Shaquille working so hard to improve. "I like his work ethic," said Scott Skiles. He's going to get better, a whole lot better, because he's not afraid to work at it."

In the pre-season, the Magic played eight exhibition games against other NBA teams. The games were a preview of the great things Shaquille could do on the court, and of the other things that he still needed to work on. There were amazing feats and embarrassing mistakes.

In his first game as a pro, an exhibition game against the Miami Heat on October 16, Shaquille scored 25 points and blocked three shots, including a booming **rejection** of Miami center Rony Seikaly's first shot of the game. But he also had nine turnovers and

> **Hoop Talk:**
> **Rejection.** A blocked shot.

had to leave the game when he became out of breath from running up and down the court.

In an exhibition game against the Charlotte Hornets, Shaquille had 26 points and 11 rebounds. One time, he blocked a shot on one end of the court to start a fast break; then he finished the play by beating everyone else downcourt for a layup. But he also lost the ball six times and was tricked into committing some silly offensive fouls.

All in all, though, Shaquille was off to a good start. In the eight exhibition games, he averaged a team-high 17.8 points and 10 rebounds while playing a little more than half of each game.

He blocked 15 shots and made 10 steals, also best on the team.

Shaquille was more than a **match for every center he played against**. Nobody could stop him once he got the ball close to the basket and made his spin move, or took his little jump shot; he was too strong and too quick. The only person who was stopping Shaquille right now was Shaquille himself, with turnovers, offensive fouls, and foul shooting that could be awful.

But win or lose, every game Shaquille played in was an event. Before the season even started, the Magic had

These five players not only showed great talent as rookies, but they helped their teams improve:

* **David Robinson** led the Spurs to 35 more wins than they had the year before he arrived and a trip to the conference semi-finals.

* **Larry Bird** led the Celtics to a 32-game improvement and a trip to the conference finals.

* **Kareem Abdul-Jabbar** led the Milwaukee Bucks to a 29-game improvement. In just their second year in the league, the Bucks went all the way to the Eastern Division finals.

* **Magic Johnson** led the Lakers to a 13-game improvement and an NBA title.

* **Michael Jordan** led the Bulls to an 11-game improvement and their first trip to the playoffs in four seasons.

sold 13,000 season tickets out of a possible 15,000 seats in the Orlando Arena. At one exhibition game in Asheville, North Carolina, fans ran onto the court to get Shaquille's autograph. After a game in South Dakota, he was mobbed by thousands of fans outside the arena, who ripped his coat to shreds. Shaquille just laughed about it.

"The NBA is fantastic," Shaquille told a group of reporters. "It's fun. I'm having a good time. I'm not worrying about anything. I'm too young to worry."

But it was time for the other NBA players and coaches to worry—about facing Shaquille. The NBA regular season was about to begin!

9
Rookie of the Year

When Wilt Chamberlain was 20 years old, he was just a sophomore at the University of Kansas. When Bill Russell was 20, he was finishing his first college basketball season at the University of San Francisco. When David Robinson was 20, he was attending the United States Naval Academy and was still four years away from the NBA. But Shaquille, at age 20, was already preparing to compete against the best basketball players in the world.

Shaquille was in no hurry to grow up. His best friends on the team were Nick Anderson and Dennis Scott, both 24 years old. They called themselves the "Knuckleheads." That nickname came from Shaquille's days at LSU. A referee in the Southeastern Conference would always tell the team captains before games, "Keep it clean, you knuckleheads."

Now whenever Shaquille, Dennis, and Nick were introduced to the crowd before a game, these new Knuckleheads would jog out with their fists raised to their foreheads, knuckles up.

Shaquille and Dennis also worked out a rap routine that they performed in the clubhouse before games. Dennis provided the beat and Shaquille did the singing.

"I'll always be a kid," Shaquille said about these antics. "Even when I'm 50 and retired, I'll still be the same person. But when it's time to play, it's time to play."

The 1992–93 NBA season began on Friday, November 6. In their first game, the Orlando Magic played the Miami Heat in Orlando. More than 180 reporters, including some from Spain, France, Japan, and Latin America, were at the opener to cover Shaquille's debut.

Although the Magic won, Shaquille's first regular season game was not as memorable as his first exhibition game. He got into early foul trouble and scored only 12 points before fouling out. Still, he showed how tough he could be, even on a bad night, by pulling down 18 rebounds. That was the most rebounds by a rookie in his first game since Bill Walton had 18 for the Portland Trail Blazers in 1974.

NBA teams have a tough schedule. They play 82 regular season games compared to just 30 for college teams. Sometimes they play three games a week, and often they have to play two nights in a row.

But Shaquille got into the NBA rhythm right away. The night after their opening game, the Magic were in Landover, Maryland, to play the Washington Bullets.

The NBA is made up of 27 teams. The teams are divided into two conferences, the Eastern Conference and the Western Conference. Each conference is divided into two divisions: the Atlantic Division and the Central Division in the Eastern Conference, and the Midwest Division and the Pacific Division in the Western Conference. The Magic play in the Atlantic Division, along with the Knicks, Nets, Celtics, 76ers, Bullets, and Heat.

Shaquille wasn't tired. All that hard work and practice in training camp had given him more endurance. He got off to a fast start and scored 16 points in the first half. He finished with 22 points and 15 rebounds as the Magic won their second game in a row.

In Game 3, against the Charlotte Hornets three days later, Shaquille had 35 points and 10 rebounds after just three quarters!

But in the fourth quarter, Shaquille developed a bad case of "rookie-itis." He had trouble getting free of the swarming Hornet defense and rushed his shots. Shaquille didn't score a single point in the last period, and the Magic lost the game.

Shaquille had his ups and downs in the first few games—but there were a lot more ups than downs. In his next game, a win over the Bullets in Orlando, Shaquille scored 31 points and grabbed 21 rebounds. A few days later, despite early foul trouble, he scored 29 points and grabbed 15 rebounds against the New Jersey Nets.

After just five games, Shaquille was first in the league in rebounding (16.4 per game), tied for fourth in scoring (25.8), and fifth in blocked shots (3.4). He was named NBA Player of the Week. It was the first time a rookie had ever won that honor in his first week in the league!

Shaquille was still trying to get better. After practice, he worked with shooting coach Buzz Braman on improving his free-throw shooting. Shaquille was making barely half of his free throws; good free-throw shooters make at least three-fourths of their shots.

Shaquille was getting fouled a lot by players who

Here's how some of the best current and past NBA centers scored and rebounded in their rookie seasons:

Center	Season	PPG	RPG
Wilt Chamberlain	1959–60	37.6	27.0
Kareem Abdul-Jabbar	1969–70	28.8	14.5
David Robinson	1989–90	24.3	12.0
Hakeem Olajuwon	1984–85	20.6	11.9
Patrick Ewing	1985–86	20.0	9.0
Bill Russell	1956–57	14.7	19.6

would push him or bump into him because they couldn't stop him from scoring any other way. Sometimes, late in a close game, they would foul him on purpose (rather than letting him take a shot) because they thought he would miss the free throws.

Meanwhile, Shaq-mania was spreading. The Magic publicity office was flooded with requests for interviews and photo sessions with Shaquille from TV stations, radio stations, newspapers, and magazines. When the Magic was on the road, Shaquille would arrive at the arena a half hour before his teammates to answer questions from all the reporters who wanted to write stories about him.

Almost everywhere Shaquille played, the game was a sellout. In Seattle, the SuperSonics had to hire extra security people to get Shaquille into the arena. In Philadelphia, the Magic used a local rap group to sneak Shaquille out of the team's hotel. In New Jersey, 50 people stood in the rain outside his hotel to catch a glimpse of Shaquille boarding the team bus. In Los Angeles, 200 people waited outside the practice gym while Shaquille and the Magic worked out.

Shaquille would high-five the fans and sign autographs whenever he could. One time, in New York, a group of kids waited for him to leave a restaurant so that they could get his autograph. When Shaquille heard about it, he invited the kids in and paid for their dinner.

Patrick Ewing has been the center for the New York Knicks since 1985. Patrick is 7' tall and weighs 240 pounds. He was the first pick in the 1985 NBA draft. He has averaged 20 or more points per game in each of his eight NBA seasons and has been selected for the All-Star team seven times.

The Magic won 8 of their first 11 games and spent all of November in first place in the Atlantic Division of the NBA. On Saturday, November 21, Shaquille and the Magic arrived in New York City to play the New York Knicks. The Knicks were favored to win the Atlantic Division, and this would be Shaquille's first game against an All-Star center, the Knicks' **Patrick Ewing**.

The Knicks were the toughest defensive team Shaquille had seen so far. They double- and triple-teamed him almost every time he touched the ball. Shaquille got a little rattled. He forced shots and threw bad passes. The referees called him for traveling and **charging**. At half time, he had just seven points and five turnovers.

Hoop Talk:
Charging. When an offensive player runs into a defensive player who is standing still. An offensive foul.

Shaquille settled down and played a little better in the second half, but the Knicks won the game easily. Still, even though Shaquille hadn't played as well as he usually did, he outscored Patrick 18 points to 15 points and out-rebounded him 17–9.

After the game, Shaquille was asked by reporters to compare himself to the Knicks' All-Star center. Shaquille was modest. "Patrick's a great player," he told them. "I'm a pretty good player."

Because of his terrific performance in the first month of the season, Shaquille was named NBA Player of the Month for November. It was the first time a rookie had won the honor in his first month in the NBA. Not bad for someone who calls himself "a pretty good player."

But that wasn't the best thing Shaquille did in November. He topped off the month by doing something for the poor people of Orlando. Shaquille had already purchased 20 season tickets to Magic games for kids whose parents couldn't afford to take them to games. This time, he gave a Thanksgiving Day dinner for 300 homeless people at a shelter in Orlando.

Shaquille came to the shelter on Thanksgiving Day. He said grace, dished out the peas and rice, and then sat down at a table to eat a turkey dinner with some of the homeless people. Afterward, he signed autographs for them and posed for photographs. When he left the shelter with the Magic's publicity man, Shaquille asked him, "What can we do for Christmas, bro?"

Shaquille was enjoying life as a professional basketball player. Because he was always being mobbed by fans, he couldn't go into many restaurants or stores. When the team was on the road, he spent a lot of time in his hotel room, ordering room service and watching hotel movies. But he wasn't complaining. "I'm having fun going from city to city, playing against All-Stars, and meeting people like Neon Deion Sanders, Denzel Washington, and Walter Payton," he said.

When the Magic traveled to Los Angeles in early December, Shaquille appeared on *The Arsenio Hall Show* again. Shaquille's favorite rap group, Fu Schnickens, was also on the show.

Shaquille asked if he could do a song with them, and the rap group said sure. So Shaquille changed from his suit into a funky red outfit. He towered over the four members of the group as they all bopped around the stage, rapping the song, "What's Up, Doc?" Shaquille was now a rap star, too!

In team sports, great players tend to help their teammates play better. That was becoming true of Shaquille and the Magic. Because their opponents had to concentrate on stopping Shaquille, his teammates were getting open for shots. And when Shaquille was double teamed, he was passing them the ball. In early December, Nick Anderson was averaging 21.5 points per game and Dennis Scott was averaging 20. Forward Jeff Turner was leading the league in field-goal percentage, and Scott Skiles was sixth in the league in assists.

Although the Magic were no longer in first place, they had become a good team, capable of beating the best teams on some nights. They had come a long way from being among the league's doormats. They even beat the two-time NBA champion Chicago Bulls— despite 64 points by Michael Jordan!

In December, the Magic won four games in a row to match their longest winning streak ever. Shaquille also thought of a good way to celebrate Christmas. He gave $1,000 toy store gift certificates to 10 needy families in the Orlando area.

As 1993 began, Shaquille continued to show that he could hold his own—and then some—against the best centers in the game. Against Robert Parish of the Boston Celtics, he had 22 points, 12 rebounds, and 4 blocks in a victory that snapped a Magic losing streak. "He's already a handful," said Robert. "Once his game becomes polished, he'll be two handfuls."

Shaquille was earning respect everywhere he played. "He made me feel like a little kid," said Brad Daugherty, All-Star center of the Cleveland Cavaliers, after a game against Shaquille. Hakeem Olajuwon, the All-Star center of the Houston Rockets, said Shaquille "reminded me of myself, only bigger."

Shaquille's battles with Patrick Ewing were becoming legendary. In one game in January against the Knicks, the Magic were down by 10 in the fourth quarter. But Shaquille led a comeback with back-to-back baskets and three blocked shots. Then Shaquille stopped Patrick on the last play of the game to give the Magic a one-point victory! Shaquille outscored Patrick 22–21 and out-rebounded him 13–12.

Then on February 14, Valentine's Day, Shaquille and the Magic went up against Patrick and the Knicks again. This time the game was so close it went into **triple overtime**!

Shaquille started off slowly in the game because of early foul trouble, but he finished with 21 points, 19 rebounds, and 9 blocked shots. Patrick had 34 points, 14 rebounds, and 4 blocks. After Patrick fouled out at the end of the first overtime, Shaquille led the Magic to victory.

But the Magic rookie wasn't just saving his best games for the Knicks. He twice had 38-point performances—against the Philadelphia 76ers and the Dallas Mavericks—and then topped that with 46 points in an overtime loss to the Detroit Pistons, just before the All-Star Game.

Hoop Talk:
Overtime. An extra five-minute period that is played after a game ends in a tie. If the overtime ends in a tie, a double overtime is played, then a triple overtime, and so on.

He had some bad games, too, but he took them in stride. After one loss, he gave reporters his best Arnold Schwarzenegger imitation. "I'll be *baaack*," Shaquille told them.

Magic general manager Pat Williams thought that in just half a season, Shaquille had already gone to the head of the class among NBA centers. But Shaquille knew he wasn't playing at his best—yet. "I think there are three great centers out there," Shaquille said. "Patrick Ewing, David Robinson, and Hakeem Olajuwon. I am not one of them yet."

10

All-Star!

Shaquille wasn't saying much about how well he was playing, but basketball fans around the country were talking non-stop about this amazing rookie.

In the NBA, fans vote for their favorite players to play in the All-Star Game on ballots that are handed out at the games. The player at each position who receives the most votes starts the game, which is played about midway through the season, in early February.

It is rare that a **rookie is named to start**. The ballots are printed early in the NBA season, before most rookies have a chance to start even for their own teams. The last rookie to start an All-Star Game was Michael Jordan in 1985.

But when the voting was over for the 1993 All-Star Game, Shaquille had 826,767 votes—more than any other center in the league! In fact, he got the fourth-largest number of votes of all the All-Stars, finishing behind only Michael Jordan, Scottie Pippen, and Charles Barkley.

Besides Shaquille, only 13 players started in the NBA All-Star Game in their rookie seasons: **Michael Jordan** (1985), **Isiah Thomas** (1982), **Magic Johnson** (1980), **Elvin Hayes** (1969), **Rick Barry** (1966), **Luke Jackson** (1965), **Jerry Lucas** (1964), **Walt Bellamy** (1962), **Oscar Robertson** (1961), **Wilt Chamberlain** (1960), **Tom Heinsohn** (1957), **Ray Felix** (1954), and **Bob Cousy** (1951).

Shaquille was named the starting center for the Eastern Conference All-Stars. He replaced Patrick Ewing, who had been the starter the past three seasons.

This news upset Patrick's coach, Pat Riley of the Knicks, who was also the coach of the Eastern Conference All-Stars. Coach Riley felt that Patrick deserved to start in the All-Star Game, and he said so.

Reporters asked Shaquille if it bothered him to hear Coach Riley say that. But Shaquille understood that Coach Riley was just standing up for one of his players. "I would never knock a man for voicing his opinion," he said. "And I'm sure that if my coach was coaching this game, he would say the same thing."

Shaquille also offered some advice to Patrick. "If I was Patrick, I wouldn't worry about it," Shaquille said.

"The All-Star Game is for the fans. If the coaches were picking, they probably would've put Patrick first and me second.

"What you can't control," Shaquille added, "you shouldn't worry about."

The NBA All-Star Game was part of a big All-Star weekend from February 19–21 in Salt Lake City, Utah, home of the Utah Jazz. During the All-Star break, NBA players get a three-day rest from playing games. The players who had not been selected to play in the All-Star Game went home to spend time with their families. The All-Stars came to Salt Lake City to practice for the game. Some players also came to compete in the other events of the weekend. Besides the All-Star Game on Sunday, there was a slam-dunk competition, a three-point shot competition, and an old-timers' game.

Shaquille did not compete in any of those competitions, but he did take part in the NBA's Stay in School Jam on Saturday afternoon. The Stay in School Jam is a big party the NBA holds every year to encourage kids to stay in school and get a good education. The stands of Salt Lake City's Delta Center arena were packed with kids, who watched entertainers and NBA players put on a show.

The rap star himself, Shaquille O'Neal, came out to sing a song with Fu Schnickens. Dressed in a black wool cap with a tassel, a leather jacket, cuffed jeans, and an "S" pendant dangling from his neck, the seven-footer bopped around the stage. The audience loved it.

Shaquille was enjoying the weekend, just like a fan. He even had his picture taken with Michael Jordan and the Charlotte Hornets' Larry Johnson and got their autographs!

On the day of the All-Star Game, Shaquille was so excited that he was the first player out of the locker room and onto the court. He cheered during warm-ups when the other stars made dunks. He even got into a dunking contest with Michael Jordan.

When it was time for the All-Stars to be introduced to the crowd, the arena lights dimmed and the spotlights came on. A television camera caught Shaquille waiting his turn on the bench, and he winked to everyone watching at home.

Starting for the Western Conference All-Stars, the announcer said, were Clyde Drexler of the Portland Trail Blazers and John Stockton of the Utah Jazz at guard, Karl Malone of the Utah Jazz and Charles Barkley of the Phoenix Suns at forward, and David Robinson of the San Antonio Spurs at center. For the Eastern Conference, it was Isiah Thomas of the Detroit Pistons and Michael Jordan at guard, Scottie Pippen of the Bulls and Larry Johnson at forward, and at center... *Shaquille O'Neal!*

The arena lights came back on when Shaquille's name was introduced, and the crowd cheered. "That was a real thrill," Shaquille said later.

Most All-Star Games are played like easy practice sessions. No one plays much defense, so the great players are allowed to show their stuff. But not this time. There was too much pride at stake. The West had beaten the East by 40 points the year before, and the East wanted to make sure that didn't happen again.

Shaquille won the center jump over **David Robinson**. The East All-Stars moved downcourt, and the ball was passed to Shaquille near the basket—usually a sure bucket for him. Shaquille went up for the shot, and *whack!* Clyde Drexler blocked the shot, but he also fouled Shaquille. Shaquille went to the line and made both free throws to give the East a 2–0 lead.

The teams moved down to the other end of the court. David Robinson took a pass about 10 feet from the basket, and before Shaquille could make a move toward him, turned and hit a jump shot to tie the score. Shaquille wasn't used to guarding seven-footers who were *that* quick!

David Robinson has been the center for the San Antonio Spurs since 1989. He is 7'1" tall and weighs 235 pounds. David won the Rookie of the Year Award and has been a four-time member of the All-Star team. He is known for his quickness and shot-blocking ability.

Shaquille came back downcourt and tried to take David to the basket. He turned and threw up a hurried shot. *Swat!* David knocked it away.

The West made its first six shots and jumped out to a 14–6 lead. But the East came roaring back with Shaquille leading the way. Shaquille launched a line-drive jump shot from the foul line. It wasn't pretty, but it went in. On defense, he scared **Hakeem Olajuwon** into throwing up a wild shot. On another play, Shaquille picked up a loose ball on a fast break, thread-ed through three defenders, slammed the ball through the basket, *and was fouled on the play!* He even made the foul shot. Shaquille came out of the game for Patrick Ewing with 3:57 left to play in the first quarter. By that time, the East was ahead 22–16.

But when Shaquille came back into the game in the second quarter, he learned something. The top centers and power forwards in the NBA were not going to stand by and let a 20-year-old rookie make them look bad.

Hakeem Olajuwon has been the center for the Houston Rockets since 1984. He is 7′ tall and weighs 255 pounds. Hakeem was born in Lagos, Nigeria. He has aver-aged 20 or more points and 11 or more rebounds in each of his nine NBA seasons.

On one play, Shaquille took a nifty alley-oop pass from Isiah Thomas and came down for the dunk. *Oof!* Shawn Kemp of the Seattle SuperSonics fouled Shaquille, but he blocked the shot. On another play, Shaquille made a spin move to get around David Robinson and then went in for the slam. Pow! Charles Barkley was there to block the shot and foul Shaquille. On still another play, Shaquille threw a good fake to shake Hakeem Olajuwon, and went up for the dunk. *Smack!* The ball was swatted away.

At halftime, the West led 57–52. It hadn't been easy for Shaquille, but he still was one of his team's leading scorers, with 13 points, and he had 6 rebounds. The TV announcers said he was a candidate to be the game's most valuable player!

But in the second half, other All-Stars got their chance to shine. Shaquille was bottled up by some good defensive play by Hakeem Olajuwon. He also spent a lot of time on the bench. Shaquille sat down midway through the third quarter and didn't return until less than two minutes remained in the fourth. Then, with just seconds to play, and the East down by two, Coach Riley wanted a center in the game with a better outside shot than Shaquille's. Patrick Ewing came in and hit a 10-foot jump shot to send the game into overtime.

In the overtime, Coach Riley tried playing both Shaquille and Patrick together, but it didn't work out.

Shaquille took only one shot—a layup—and missed it. Led by John Stockton and Karl Malone, the West won the game 135-130.

After such a good start, Shaquille finished with 14 points and 7 rebounds—only one more point and one more rebound than he'd had at halftime. And he had no blocked shots. Reporters asked Shaquille if he was disappointed that he hadn't played more. "No, not really," he said. "I guess Pat Riley wanted more experience in the game down the stretch."

Shaquille said that was all right with him. "I had fun," he said. "I'm just glad to be here." He had also earned more respect from his peers.

"He's tough. He's big. He has strength," said Hakeem Olajuwon. "He can play against anybody."

David Robinson, who had played against Shaquille for the first time, said: "He's everything everyone said he was."

On March 6, 1993, Shaquille O'Neal turned 21 years old. Shaquille was just a little more than midway through his first season in the NBA, but he had already accomplished much of what everybody had expected of him. And everyone had been expecting so much.

He had taken a bad team and made it into a solid NBA club. Every team in the league, including the Chicago Bulls and the Phoenix Suns, knew it was in for a battle any time it had to face Shaquille and the Orlando Magic.

Before Shaquille joined the team, the most games that the Magic had ever won in a season was 31. With Shaquille, the team broke that record in late March.

The Magic finished the season with a 41–41 record and just missed making the playoffs. Orlando won 20 games more in 1992–93 than it had in 1991–92—the biggest improvement of any team in the NBA!

Orlando not only was good, the team was lucky, too. The Magic topped off the season by winning the NBA draft lottery (for the number-one pick in the draft) for the second year in a row. The odds against Orlando winning were 66–1.

Shaquille, meanwhile, proved himself to be one of the great players in the league. He finished the season ranked eighth in the NBA in scoring, with 23.4 points per game; second in rebounding, with 13.9 per game; second in blocks, with 3.53 per game; and fourth in field-goal percentage, with a .562 mark. He broke the Magic team record for blocked shots (83) after just 26 games, and set team records in scoring, rebounding, and shooting accuracy.

Shaquille was voted NBA Rookie of the Year. He also received a few votes in the balloting for the league's **Most Valuable Player** award, which went to Charles Barkley of the Phoenix Suns. And even though the Magic didn't make the playoffs, Shaquille was on TV for 48 minutes during the first weekend of the playoffs— on commercials! With his spectacular dunks, rap singing, and commercials, Shaquille had become one of

Only two players have ever been named Rookie of the Year and Most Valuable Player in their rookie seasons: **Wilt Chamberlain** and **Wes Unseld**. Wilt averaged 37.6 points per game and 27 rebounds for the Philadelphia Warriors in the 1959–60 season. Wes, who is now coach of the Washington Bullets, averaged 13.8 points and 18.2 rebounds for the Bullets in 1968–69.

the NBA's most popular players—right up there with Michael Jordan!

Most of all, though, Shaquille had accomplished all that while still living up to his expectations of himself. Money had not changed him as a person. He was generous in sharing his new wealth, with the homeless and needy families, and his time, with kids and fans. He also continued to make sure he had fun both on and off the court.

Shaquille had come a long way from that clumsy 13-year-old with no friends who was always getting into trouble with his teachers and his parents. But he hadn't forgotten how he got from there to where he is today.

Shaquille says he will take correspondence courses

next year or attend summer school so that he can receive his college diploma. That is a promise he has made to his mom and dad.

"At our house you see a wall when you walk in that has plaques and awards and stuff that my sisters and brother and me have gotten," he says. "There's an empty place on the wall right next to my kindergarten and high school diploma. Dad says that space is for my college degree."

He continues to be close to his parents. They are, he says, his role models. "When I was a kid, I could look up to Doctor J," he says, "but if I needed some advice, I couldn't ask Doctor J. I had to call Mommy or Daddy."

And he plans to keep working hard to become the best player he can be.

"I was taught to just go play and play hard and that's what made me who I am today," Shaquille says. "Maybe one day I'll be considered great, or maybe one day I'll be in the Hall of Fame. If not, I'm always going to keep on smiling."

That's what being Shaquille O'Neal is all about.